Andrea Assenzio-Chaisson

*Our
Family
Favorites
Cookbook*

ISBN-13: 978-0-615-26281-9

OUR FAMILY FAVORITES COOKBOOK

Copyright © 2008 by Andrea Assenzio-Chaisson

All rights reserved.

Printed in U.S.A.

Our Family Favorites Cookbook is Dedicated to Florence Manca (Grandma)

Grandma was ahead of her time in the kitchen, she made frittatas when they were called omelets, she kept the traditions for all the holidays and she even made corned beef and cabbage on St. Patrick's Day, which was really a novelty in an Italian household. She made meatballs on Sunday morning, so you could have a meatball sandwich for breakfast (even though she made them at the crack of dawn, they were kept warm for you until you got up). Many of the recipes in this cookbook are hers, the rest are ones that have become our favorites - some old, some new that we picked up from other family members and friends along the way.

A Short Family History

Martino Manca (Grandpa) came to the United States in 1911 from Theisi, Sardinia, landing in New York. He traveled across the country stopping in Vancouver Canada and San Francisco. In San Francisco he worked on the railroad and construction, you will see some pictures in this book of him in San Francisco and pictures my mom, sister, daughter and I took in San Francisco while we were there looking for the places he always talked about. In 1925 he went back east to Greenwich, Connecticut where he met and married Mary Strazza, a widow with one son Michael Carlo (Uncle Mike). Martino and Mary had two daughters Anna (Mom) and Marie (Aunt Marie). Martino and his brother built a house in Greenwich, Connecticut to raise their children in. Unfortunately the depression came and took the house away, so the families moved to the east side of Manhattan where Martino opened a fruit store. Again tragedy strikes and Mary dies of cancer in 1940 leaving her husband and her three children. In time Martino married Florence Capozzi (Grandma) and they buy the "Farm" (pictured on the cover) in Highland, New York. Martino & Florence have one son Andrew (Uncle Andrew).

Michael Carlo married Gertrude Restaino (Aunt Gertie) and have three children, Mary Jo, Michele and Martin
Mary Jo married Russ Mann – Mary Jo has two sons Michael and Christopher
Michele married Robert Breed
Martin married Alicia and have two sons, Martino and Angelo

Marie Manca married Al Short (Uncle Al) and have three children, Alan, Mary and Ronald
Alan married Suzanne and have one son Mel
Mary married David Hartsek and have two daughters Julia and Katie
Ronnie passed away when he was 18 years old, he will always be lovingly remembered

Anna Manca (Mom) married Santo Assenzio (Dad) and have three children, Mary Ann, Andrea and Thomas
Mary Ann married Vincent Serio and have one son, Alex
Andrea married David Chaisson - Andrea has two children, Thomas Martin and Kerry Ann
Thomas Martin married Caroline Theye and have one daughter, Isabella
Thomas married Josie Ianniello and have three children, Thomas, Samantha and Christina

Andrew Manca married Carolyn and have three sons, Andrew, Christopher and Daniel
Andrew married Jody Magnani
Christopher married Jennifer Elliott

The Sidewalks of New York

Our family contributed to the bustling Italian immigrant section of Manhattan's Lower East Side in the early 20th Century with some of the most delectable treats around. The recipes have survived through the generations, and we are now offering a few of our favorites to you.

In the early 20th Century, immigrants were flooding into Ellis Island from all over the world. Each ethnicity setup a little piece of home in a different section of New York. My ancestors found themselves in what came to be know as "Little Italy" located on the Lower East Side of Manhattan.

Within Little Italy, food stores and pushcarts lined the sidewalks. The stores specialized in different types of food, the meat store, vegetable store, dairy, etc. Food was bought on a daily basis to make dinner for the evening meal, guaranteeing a fresh and tasty dinner.

My family had a variety of stores in Little Italy. Alfonso Capozzi made and sold calzone's in a store on the corner of 114th Street and First Avenue. Martino Manca owned a fruit store next door. You could stop at Jimmy Restaino's hot dog cart for lunch and then treat yourself to a donut ala mode at Julio & Margaret Dore's Ice Cream Parlor.

We hope you enjoy our recipes as much as we do!
Thank you

Thank you to our wonderful family without their help this book could not be possible

2221 First Avenue Manhattan, New York (1930's)

Dad (left) while in the Navy 1950's

Table of Contents

	Page
### Holiday Menu's	14

Appetizers

Zucchini with Onions	20
Seven Layer Dip	21
Bruschetta	22
Clam Dip	23
Artichoke/Spinach Dip	24
David's Chicken Wings	25
Steamed Spiced Shrimp	26

Main Dishes

Capellini with Artichokes, Capers, Tomatoes and Fish of the Day	28
Linguine with White Clam Sauce	29
Homemade Manicotti	30
Dave's Chili	31
Pork Daube	32
Linguine with Gorgonzola, Prosciutto, & Fresh Spinach	33
Italian Meat Pie	34

Shrimp Parmigiano	*35*
Fried Flounder Filet	*36*
Zuppa di Pesce	*37*
Carbonara	*38*
Meatballs & Sauce	*39*
Chicken Wings with Wine	*40*
Chicken Soup	*41*
Spedini	*42*
Chicken Cacciatore	*43*
Chinese Chicken with Rice	*44*
Chicken Marsala	*45*
Braised Pork Chops with Mushrooms & Onions	*46*
Spaghetti alla Genovese	*47*
Lasagna	*48*
Macaroni & Cheese	*49*
Vinnie's Scarpariello	*50*
Cauliflower with Macaroni	*51*
Lentil Soup	*52*
Spaghetti with Shrimp & Asparagus	*53*
Rack of Lamb	*54*
Steamed Maryland Crabs	*55*

Grilled Hot Sausage & Peppers   *56*
Grits with Gouda Cheese &
    Italian Sausage   *57*
Eggplant, Mozzarella Cheese & Portobello
    Mushroom Pannini   *58*
Chicken Cutlet Parmigiano   *59*

Side Dishes

Stuffed Calamari	*62*
Josephine's Spinach Pie	*63*
Stuffed Clams	*64*
Steamed Clams	*65*
Vienna's Sausage Stuffing	*66*
Potato Croquettes	*67*
Ollie's Potato Salad	*68*
Seafood Salad	*69*
Polpo	*70*
Whiting Salad (fish)	*71*
Asparagus	*72*
Beef Braciole	*73*
Onions for Hot Dogs	*74*
Italian Potato Salad	*75*
Grandma's Potato & Eggs	*76*

Giambotta	*77*
Broccoli Rabe	*78*
Fried Cauliflower	*79*
Rice Stuffing	*80*
Stuffed Peppers	*81*
Broccoli Casserole	*82*
Pasta Salad	*83*
Corn Pudding	*84*
Panzanella	*85*
Fresh Mozzarella, Tomatoes & Basil Salad	*86*
Orange Salad	*87*
Cucumber Salad	*88*
Tortellini & Spinach Salad	*89*

<u>All Holiday's</u>

Antipasto for Holiday's	*92*
Roasted Peppers	*93*
Caponata	*94*
Rice Balls (Arancini)	*95*
Stuffed Mushrooms	*96*
Stuffed Artichokes	*97*
Eggplant Parmigiano	*98*

Breads

Irish Soda Bread	*100*
Braided Easter Bread	*101*
Pumpkin Bread	*102*
Easter Bread	*103*

Desserts

Rugelach	*106*
Marianne's Nut Cookies	*107*
Jewel Cookies	*108*
Bows	*109*
Struffoli	*110*
Creamy Rice Pudding	*111*
Chocolate Pudding Pie	*112*
Italian Honey Twists	*113*
Taralles	*114*
Pumpkin Pie	*115*
Sock-it-to-me-Cake	*116*
Applesauce Cake	*117*
Fresh Apple Pie	*118*

Wines   *119*

Christmas Eve Menu

We always start our Christmas Eve celebration with a Brandy Alexander
1 oz Creame de' Cocoa
1 oz Heavy cream
1 oz Brandy
Shake well with ice
Strain into glass – sprinkle with nutmeg

Wine is served throughout the meal

Appetizers

Antipasto
Cheeses – Mozzarella, Extra Sharp Provolone
Caponata
Roasted Peppers
Seafood Salad
Shrimp Cocktail
Polpo
Stuffed Mushrooms
Italian Bread

Main Course

Fruiti di Mare con Linguini
Shrimp Parmigiano
Baked Halibut
Lobster Tails
Fried Breaded Flounder Filet
Stuffed Calamari
Eggplant Parmigiano
Broccoli Rabe
Stuffed Artichokes

After Dinner

Anise (Fennel)
Nuts & Fruit

Dessert

Black Coffee w/Anisette
Italian Pastries
Struffoli
Jewel Cookies
Nut Crescent Cookies

After Dinner Drink

Port

Midnight

Fried Italian Sausage
(For good luck)

Thanksgiving Menu

* Wine is served throughout the meal*

Appetizers

Antipasto
Stuffed Mushrooms
Cheeses – Mozzarella, Extra Sharp Provolone
Meats – Soppressata, Prosciutto, Capicola, Hard Salami
Caponata
Roasted Peppers
Clam Dip
Italian Bread

Main Course

Turkey
Rice Stuffing
Eggplant Parmigiano
Stuffed Artichokes
Butternut Squash
Sweet Potatoes
Baked Potatoes
Broccoli Casserole
Fried Cauliflower

Dessert

Black Coffee w/Anisette
Home-made Pumpkin Pie
Home-made Apple Pie
Italian Pastries

Easter Menu

* Wine is served throughout the meal*

Appetizers

Antipasto
Stuffed Mushrooms
Caponata
Roasted Peppers
Cheeses – Mozzarella, Extra Sharp Provolone
Meats - Soppressata, Prosciutto, Capicola, Hard Salami
Italian Bread

Main Course

Rack of Lamb
Spedini
Asparagus
Eggplant Parmigiano
Stuffed Artichokes
Rice Balls
Green Salad

Dessert

Italian Pastries

Our family trip to Theisi, Sardinia, 1975
Right – Babautz (Godfather) at a picnic on the family farm in Theisi
Top left – At Capo Testa Restaurant in Castlesarda, Sardinia
Bottom left – the family walking to the Grotto

Appetizers

Anna enjoying Dungeness crab on the Wharf in San Francisco

Zucchini with Onions

Ingredients

2 large onions - sliced
4 zucchini – peeled, cut in half, sliced long ways
½ cup fresh mint leaves
¼ cup olive oil
¼ cup red wine vinegar
Salt & pepper to taste

❧ Fry onions in olive oil.
When onions are translucent, add a little red wine vinegar and simmer.
Fry zucchini until just brown.
Layer zucchini, onions and mint in a shallow dish.
Serve at room temperature
Serves 4

Andrea with her children – Tom & Kerry

Seven Layer Dip

Ingredients

1 16-oz can refried beans
1 8-oz tub Avocado Guacamole Dip
1 8-oz container sour cream
1 8-oz jar mayonnaise
1 1.25-oz package taco seasoning mix
2 tomatoes - chopped
2 bunches green onions - chopped
1 8-oz package grated taco blend cheese
1 4.25-oz can black olives – chopped

❧ Mix sour cream, mayonnaise and taco spice in small bowl. Layer ingredients, starting with refried beans and ending with grated taco blend cheese.
(I usually use a thin pizza pan)
Serves 6 - 8

Anna dressed for a night on the town

Bruschetta

Ingredients

6 plum tomatoes (ripe & firm)
1 medium sized Vidalia onion
5 Tbsp olive oil
Fresh basil – 8 leaves
Oregano – dash
Salt & pepper to taste
French bread

✺ Dice tomatoes and onion.
Mix together with all other ingredients.
Serve with thin slices of French bread (toast bread if desired).
Serves 4

Mary Ann in Theisi at the family picnic

Clam Dip

Ingredients

1 10.5-oz can Progresso white clam sauce
1 tsp lemon juice
1 small onion chopped
1 tsp parsley flakes
½ stick salted butter
1 clove garlic, crushed
1 tsp oregano
½ cup seasoned breadcrumbs
1 8-oz package Mozzarella cheese – shredded

❧ Simmer clam sauce and lemon juice for 5 minutes.
Add onion, garlic, parsley, butter and oregano.
Add breadcrumbs.
Place in shallow baking dish and cover with mozzarella.
Bake at 350° for 20 minutes.
Serves 4 - 6

The Assenzio Grandchildren

Artichoke/Spinach Dip

Ingredients

1 can (14 oz) Progresso artichoke hearts in water
1 16-oz package baby spinach
1 8-oz whole milk mozzarella (Polly-o)
3 Tbsp grated cheese
1 Tbsp oil
2 small cloves garlic, chopped

✑ Steam spinach and chop; sauté in oil and garlic.
Drain and squeeze artichokes, then chop.
Grate mozzarella.
Add all ingredients together and mix well.
Bake at 350° for 20 minutes or until bubbly.
Serves 4

Dave at the top of Mount Washington, 2004

David's Chicken Wings

Ingredients

3 lbs Chicken wings – cut in half at joint (discard tips)
½ cup Worcestershire sauce
½ cup red wine
¼ cup hot sauce
¼ stick salted butter
1 large onion – diced

❧ Take chicken wings, Worcestershire, red wine, onion and hot sauce – mix well, put in baking pan and let marinate in the refrigerator for at least 1 hour.

❧ Cut butter into slices distribute evenly over wings.
Put in preheated 400° oven, bake for 1 ½ hours – stirring occasionally.
Sprinkle additional hot sauce while cooking – to taste.

❧ Serve with celery sticks, carrot sticks and blue cheese dressing
Serves 4

Steamed Spiced Shrimp

Ingredients
2 lbs large shrimp
½ cup water
½ cup red apple cider vinegar
½ can beer
3 bay leaves
1 Tbsp whole peppercorns
4 Tbsp old bay seasoning

❧ In bottom of steamer pot put water, vinegar, beer, (2) bay leaves and peppercorns.

❧ In steamer basket layer shrimp sprinkling old bay seasoning in between layers, also add a couple of peppercorns and 1 bay leaf.

❧ Cover and bring to boil, add basket of shrimp and steam until shrimp are fully cooked and pink, approximately 10 minutes.

❧ Mix once while steaming

❧ Cocktail sauce – 4-oz ketchup and 2-oz horseradish – mix well
Serves 4 - 6

Main Dishes

Easter Dinner (Rack of Lamb, Rice Ball, Spedini & Asparagus)

Capellini with Artichokes, Capers, Tomatoes and Fish of the Day

Ingredients

¼ cup chopped onion
6-8 cloves of garlic, minced or smashed
2 Tbsp olive oil
1 28-oz can of plum tomatoes (including the juice), chopped
  (or 6-8 medium sized fresh plum tomatoes, chopped)
1 6-oz jar of marinated artichoke hearts, drained, chopped
2 Tbsp drained bottled capers
1 tsp dried oregano
1 Tbsp dried basil
½ tsp ground coriander
1 cup dry white wine
1 lb shrimp, scallops or any other white fish
1 lb Capellini (can also use Vermicelli or Linguini)

❦ In a large deep skillet, add olive oil and sauté onion and garlic over moderately low heat.
Stir occasionally until onion is soft - add tomatoes.
Slightly raise heat and simmer for 5 minutes.
(If using fresh tomatoes, simmer for a few minutes longer or until the tomatoes are soft)

Now is the time to start the Capellini.
In a large pot of boiling water, add Capellini.
(Things go very quickly from this point so be prepared or you will over cook your pasta! The thicker pastas require more time to cook - check the package.)

To skillet, add artichoke hearts, capers and spices.
(If using fresh oregano or basil, use twice the amount as prescribed above)
Simmer for 5 minutes.
Push tomato mixture to sides, forming a circle in center of pan.
Add wine to center.
As wine starts to bubble, add fish and then turn off heat.
(The secret to cooking fish is to cover it with wine and then just barely cook it. Feel free to add more wine if the sauce seems dry.)

Drain Capellini, saving some of the pasta water.
Place Capellini in large pasta bowl and add fish sauce.
Lightly toss Capellini.
(The pasta will absorb some of the liquid. If too dry, add up to one cup of pasta water.)
Serve pasta with grated Parmigiano.
Serves 4 - 6

Linguine with White Clam Sauce

Ingredients

2 dozen Cherrystone clams – washed, shucked and chopped (reserve clam juice)
½ cup olive oil
½ stick salted butter (optional)
1 8-oz bottle clam juice
1 head of garlic
Handful fresh parsley – chopped
Black pepper to taste
Few crushed red pepper flakes
¾ - 1 lb Linguine

ஃ Slice garlic very thin and sauté in bottled clam juice until very soft. Add chopped clams with juice, olive oil and butter into clam juice and garlic.
Simmer for 4 minutes; add parsley and black and red pepper to taste.
Serve over linguine.

Serves 4

Aunt Gertie's Homemade Manicotti

Manicotti with Italian Sausage and Salad with Balsamic Vinaigrette Dressing

Crepes
1 cup flour
1 beaten egg in 1 cup water
1/8 tsp salt
1 Tbsp cornstarch

❧ In a bowl sift dry ingredients.
Stir in egg/water mixture - batter will be thin
Spray or oil 8" skillet - medium heat - spoon 3 Tbsp batter into pan - rotate quickly to cover bottom of pan.
Cook until light brown - one side only - remove with spatula.
Stack crepes in platter (will not stick) cover with clean cloth, fill immediately or refrigerate.
Makes 8 crepes

Ricotta filling
1 15-oz container ricotta or 2 cups
½ tsp nutmeg or cinnamon
2 eggs lightly beaten
½ cup grated Parmesan cheese
½ cup shredded fresh mozzarella
¼ tsp garlic powder
2 Tbsp finely chopped fresh parsley or 1 tsp dried parsley
1/8 tsp black pepper

❧ Mix ingredients in bowl - blend together.
Use 2 - 3 Tbsp to fill each crepe - roll up crepe.
Place in baking pan - pour light tomato sauce on top.
Use 2 cups fresh sauce or a good "jar" sauce diluted with 1 cup water.
Sprinkle ¼ cup Parmesan cheese and ¼ cup shredded mozzarella on top.
Cover with tinfoil and bake at 375° for 3/4 hour. Serve with extra sauce and cheese.
Serves 4

Dave at Laconia Bike Week in New Hampshire, 2004

Dave's Chili

Ingredients

2 lbs ground beef
1 large onion – diced
2 16-oz cans whole tomatoes – cut up
2 1.25-oz packages chili seasoning
1 16-oz can pinto beans
1 16-oz can red kidney beans
6 medium size cherry peppers – remove seeds and dice
1 cup water
Ground black pepper to taste
Hot sauce to taste

❧ Combine beans with juice, cherry peppers, tomatoes, ½ onion, water and seasoning in large pot – bring to boil stirring well.
Brown ground beef with ½ onion – drain fat.
Stir ground beef mixture into bean mixture, bring to boil, stir well and simmer for about 1 ½ to 2 hours.

❧ Add hot sauce and black pepper to taste while simmering
Serves 8

Pork Daube

This recipe originally called for using Ostrich but works well using Pork Tenderloins.

1 Package of Pork Tenderloins (2)
1/2 cup of dry red wine
1 tub of veal demi glace
1/2 cup of chicken, beef, or vegetable stock
2 tablespoons olive oil
1 large onion thinly slices
2 cloves of garlic thinly sliced
3 carrots, peeled and sliced into big pieces
2 sprigs fresh thyme
Juice of 1/2 orange
Orange peel from 1/2 an orange, cut in thin strips
1 cup grape tomatoes, halved
Salt and pepper

❧ Preheat oven to 250°
Wash the tenderloins and pat dry.
In a large heavy bottom pot or dutch oven, add the olive oil and brown the pork tenderloins. When done, remove from pot and add sliced onion, carrots, and garlic and sauté until onion starts to soften. Return the pork to the pan, add the wine, demiglace, stock, thyme, orange juice and 1/2 of the orange peel. Bring the liquid to a simmer, cover with lid and place in the oven for one hour.
At the end of the hour, remove from the oven and set aside. Remove the pork and the vegetables to a warm dish and cover.
Remove the thyme and orange peel from the pot - as much as you can.
Return the pot to the stove and bring to a boil reducing the liquid to half of what you started with.
Now is time to slice up the tenderloins.
Add the tomatoes to the pot about 1 minute. Add salt and pepper to taste.
Twist the remaining orange peel over the pot and add to the sauce.
Serve the pork with portions of the onion, carrot, and tomato, spooning some sauce over the platter or each portion.

Serves 6

Linguine with Gorgonzola, Prosciutto, and Fresh Spinach

❧ With Spring in the air, any recipe with fresh baby spinach or asparagus is a real treat. The following Linguine recipe comes from the August 1996 issue of Gourmet and describes a wonderful and easy-to-make dish served at the Café Phoenix in Wilmington, NC. (Serves four.)

1 lb linguine
1 lb fresh spinach (coarse stems discarded, leaves washed well and spun dry)
1/2 lb thinly sliced Prosciutto, cut into small pieces
3-4 good-sized cloves of garlic finely chopped
2 Tbsp chopped fresh basil or 1 tablespoon dried basil
2 Tbsp chopped fresh oregano or 1 tablespoon dried oregano
3/4 cup olive oil
1/2 lb Gorgonzola, crumbled
1/2 cup pine nuts, toasted until golden (the nuts are really optional)

❧ Start the water boiling for the linguine. Cut half of the spinach leaves into thin strips. Arrange the rest of the spinach on four diner plates.

In a large heavy skillet, add 1/2 cup of oil, the Prosciutto, garlic, basil and oregano. Cook over moderately high heat, stirring, until lightly browned, about 3 minutes. Add the pasta to the boiling water and cook until al dente. Drain in colander. In the pasta bowl, toss the pasta with the remaining ¼ cup of oil, Prosciutto mixture, cut spinach and Gorgonzola. Season to taste with salt and pepper. Mound pasta on top of leaves on the dinner plates. (The heat of the pasta will continue to cook the spinach on the plate.) Garnish with basil leaves, Parmesan cheese, and pine nuts.

Asparagus - Springtime of the year you can get those very tasty and pencil-thin asparagus. Take one bunch, wash, trim ends, and shake dry. Place on a shallow jellyroll-baking pan. Drizzle on 2 tablespoons of olive oil. Sprinkle on 2-3 cloves of finely chopped garlic. Place under broiler in the oven. Turn frequently; roast until the stems are soft. Some of the stems will get a little crispy. Serve hot or room temperature.

Serves 4 - 6

Italian Meat Pie

For a 12 inch pie

Pastry
3 cups all purpose flour
¾ cup softened butter
½ tsp salt
2 small eggs lightly beaten
1 tsp baking powder
2 Tbsp water
1 egg beaten to brush

Filling
1 ½ cup Ricotta
½ lb Provolone cheese - sliced
1 lb Mozzarella cheese diced
1 2/3 cups grated Parmesan cheese
3 eggs lightly beaten
½ lb dry sausage - sliced
½ lb prosciutto – cut up
3 sprigs parsley - chopped

Pastry
In small bowl beat eggs, butter and water. Sift together flour, baking powder and salt in medium bowl. Make well in center, pour in egg mixture and stir with fork until blended. Turn dough onto board and cover with bowl for 10 minutes. Then knead until smooth. Wrap in wax paper and refrigerate until ready to use.
Preheat oven to 400º.
Lightly grease one 12-inch flat pan.
Roll out ½ of the dough to a 13-inch circle and place in pan trimming the edges (reserve).
Mix raw eggs, ricotta and grated cheese in small bowl – mix well.
Spoon mixture on pastry then arrange the rest of the ingredients on pastry – top with parsley.
Roll trimmings ½ inch thick with a cookie cutter, cut out 8 leaves.
Roll remaining pastry into 12-inch circle, trim edge. Place pastry on top of filling. Fold edge of top crust under bottom, press together to seal, crimp.
Make slits near center for steam vents, arrange leaves on top.
Brush with egg.
Bake at 370º for approximately 1 hour
Serves 8 - 10

Anna & Santo in Italy

<u>Shrimp Parmigiano</u>

Ingredients

18 jumbo shrimp
1 egg
1 cup breadcrumbs (flavored)
1 cup oil
1 8-oz package mozzarella cheese (thinly sliced)
2 cups tomato sauce

❧ Clean and de-vein shrimp.
Butterfly shrimp by cutting the back until you can spread open.
Dip shrimp in egg and breadcrumb.
Fry in oil until golden.
Remove from pan, drain excess oil.
Place in shallow baking pan, spoon sauce over each shrimp.
Add mozzarella to top of shrimp.
Bake at 350° for 10 minutes or until cheese has melted.
Serves 6

Aunt Angie, Grandma, Aunt Marie, Dad, Mom, Aunt Connie & Aunt Marie

Fried Flounder Filet

Ingredients

6 flounder filets, rinsed and dried
1 cup flour
1 cup breadcrumbs, flavored
1 egg
½ cup milk

☙ Beat egg and milk together.
Dredge flounder in flour.
Dip in egg mixture.
Coat with breadcrumbs.
Fry in oil at medium heat, until browned.
Serve immediately
Serves 2 - 4

The family picnic – Theisi, Sardinia

Zuppa di Pesce

Ingredients

12 little Neck clams, fresh – scrubbed
1 lobster, cut up – cleaned
12 shrimp, medium sized – cleaned
12 mussels – scrubbed
1 lb squid – cleaned & cut up
¼ cup olive oil
3 32-oz cans Italian tomato sauce
1 cup clam juice, bottled
1 cup white wine
1 tsp oregano
Sprig fresh basil
Salt and pepper
1 tsp parsley
5 cloves garlic, crushed
1 lb Spaghetti or Linguini

❧ Heat oil in large saucepan; add garlic, lobster, tomato sauce, clam juice, wine and oregano.
Bring to a boil, lower heat and simmer about 10 minutes.
Add other fish and cook 10 minutes longer.
Cover and cook until clams and mussels have opened – about 5 minutes.
Stir in basil, salt and pepper; toss in parsley.
Serve over Spaghetti or Linguini.
Discard any shellfish that does not open / Serves 4 - 6

Carbonara

Ingredients

Beaten egg is the secret of this delicate and delicious sauce; it coats the pasta and causes the bits of cheese and meat to cling evenly. Carbonara makes a dramatic entrée when assembled at the table. It can also be served as a first course, if you like – then it serves 6 – 8

¼ pound mild Italian pork sausage
½ pound prosciutto (finely chopped) or cooked ham (thinly sliced)
2 Tbsp butter or margarine
½ cup lightly packed minced parsley
3 eggs, beaten
½ cup freshly grated or shredded Parmigiano cheese
Pepper, to taste
About ½ lb hot, cooked and drained Tagliarini or Spaghetti
Additional grated or shredded Parmigiano cheese

Remove casings from sausage; crumble sausage. Place wok* over medium heat. When wok is hot, add sausage and half the prosciutto; stir-fry for about 5 minutes or until lightly browned. Blend remaining half of prosciutto with cooked sausage mixture; remove wok from heat.

(If you like, the following steps can be completed at the table. Have ready, in separate containers, butter, parsley, eggs, and the ½ cup cheese, as well as a pepper mill)

Add hot Tagliarini, butter, and parsley to meats. Mix quickly to blend.
At once pour in eggs and continue to blend. Quickly lifting and mixing the pasta to coat well with egg. Sprinkle in the ½ cup cheese and a dash of pepper; mix again.
Serve with additional cheese.
Makes 4 servings.

* It works in an electric frying pan too
Serves 2 - 4

Meatballs

Ingredients

1 lb ground round
2 slices of white bread (remove crust and wet)
1 cup bread crumbs (wet thoroughly)
2 large eggs
4 heaping Tbsp Romano grated cheese
2 Tbsp grated or chopped onion
1 tsp garlic powder
1 tsp parsley flakes
Salt and pepper, to taste
½ cup olive oil

❧ *Mix together; form into medium sized balls; fry in hot oil until browned.*

Tomato Sauce with Meat

Ingredients

1 slab of baby back ribs (cut in pieces of 2)
2 Tbsp Oil
1 tsp garlic powder
1 tsp basil leaves (dry)
2 cans (16 oz. each) of tomato sauce (puree)

❧ *Brown baby back ribs in oil. Add garlic powder, basil and tomato sauce. Simmer until done.*

** For a simple Marinara Sauce – omit meat**

Chicken Wings with Wine

Ingredients

3 lbs chicken wings – washed and any hairs removed
(cut into drumsticks, discarding ends)
Salt
Pepper
Paprika
½ cup olive oil
1 medium onion, diced
½ cup red wine

⁓ *Sprinkle chicken wings with salt, pepper and paprika – on both sides.*
Fry in oil until done.
In the same oil used to fry the chicken, brown the onion and pour in the red wine.
Return the chicken wings into the onion/wine mixture; reheat.
When done, pour wine mixture over wings.
Serves 4

Grandpa, Grandma & Uncle Andrew at his High School Graduation

Chicken Soup

Ingredients

6 chicken thighs
Bunch of fresh carrots – cut in pieces
Bunch of fresh celery – cut in 1 inch pieces
Sprig of parsley
2 large onions – chopped
2 chicken bouillon cubes
2 beef bouillon cubes
3 quarts water
Pepper to taste
Salt to taste

In large pot, place chicken and water, bring to boil. As it boils, keep skimming fat off the top. When you have removed all of the fat, add celery, carrots, parsley, onions and bouillon cubes.
Bring to boil.
Lower heat and simmer about 2 hours, water can be added if needed.
Remove chicken from bones and shred – return to pot.

Serve with Orzo or egg noodles
Serves 4 - 6

Spedini
(Stuffed Rolled Veal)

Ingredients

2 lbs veal cutlets, thinly sliced & cut in strips
1 cup flavored breadcrumbs
1 8-oz can tomato sauce
3 Tbsp grated cheese
1 Tbsp oil
2 large onions, sliced

❧ *Pound and slice cutlets into 1 ½ inch strips.*
In a small frying pan, mix tomato sauce, breadcrumbs and cheese in oil and sauté. (Add more breadcrumbs if needed, should be moist, but not runny.)
Place strips of veal on cutting board and spread mixture on top of each one.
Roll cutlets and place on skewers, alternate with sliced onion.
Brush with oil and bake for 15 minutes at 375°.
Turn oven to broil and broil 3 minutes on each side.
Serves 6

Grandma holding Mary Ann at the farm

Chicken Cacciatore

Ingredients

1 chicken fryer, cut in 8 pieces
1 16-oz can tomato sauce
1 large onion - sliced
2 cloves garlic, crushed
1 green and 1 red pepper – sliced
1 8-oz can sliced mushrooms
8 basil leaves
Dash oregano
Salt & pepper, to taste
1 cup white wine
1 cup flour
4 Tbsp olive oil

❧ Combine flour with salt, pepper and oregano; dredge chicken in mixture.
Heat oil in a large frying pan and fry chicken until golden brown, remove chicken and set aside.
Fry onion and peppers in the same pan until translucent.
Add garlic, tomato sauce, wine, mushrooms and basil – let simmer for 10 minutes.
Add chicken and simmer 30 minutes.
Serve over rice or with spaghetti and crusty Italian bread.

Serves 4

Chinese Chicken with Rice

Ingredients

2 large boneless chicken breasts – cut into 1-inch pieces.
1 package Lipton onion soup mix
1 Tbsp soy sauce
1 Tbsp cornstarch

❧ Mix above ingredients together and marinate chicken.

---

2 Onions, chopped
1 head Celery, cut in 1" pieces
2 bunches Scallions, halved
2 large Green pepper, cut in slices

❧ Add vegetables to a frying pan or wok and sauté until translucent.
Remove vegetables and add chicken.
Sauté chicken, until done.

Mix together
1 cup water
1 Tbsp soy sauce
1 Tbsp sugar
2 Tbsp cornstarch

❧ When chicken is done, add water and corn starch mixture.
Add vegetables and cook until tender.
Serve over rice.
Serves 4

Anna & Marie – My Sister My Best Friend

Chicken Marsala

Ingredients

3 Tbsp flour
½ tsp salt
¼ tsp pepper
4 5-oz boneless chicken breasts
2 Tbsp butter
1 Tbsp oil
6-oz sliced mushrooms
¼ cup Marsala wine
¼ cup beef broth
2 tsp cornstarch

❧ Combine flour, salt and pepper.
Dredge chicken in mixture to coat.
Heat one tablespoon butter and one tablespoon oil in skillet.
Add chicken to skillet and brown; remove and drain chicken on paper towel.
Add remaining butter. Sauté mushrooms, remove when soft.
Add Marsala to skillet to deglaze pan. Remove from heat.
Whisk broth and cornstarch in bowl until smooth; add to Marsala in skillet.
Return chicken and mushrooms to skillet. Spoon broth mixture over top.
Simmer until sauce gets thick and heated through.
Serves 4

Braised Pork Chops with Mushrooms & Onions

Ingredients

2 Tbsp oil
2 large onions – halved & sliced
1 carrot – peeled & thinly sliced
2 cloves garlic – minced
6-oz mushrooms – sliced
½ cup white wine
½ tsp salt
1 tsp dried rosemary
¼ tsp sage
4 loin-cut pork chops (5 oz each)

❧ In a 12" skillet, heat the oil over low heat.
Add onions to pan and sauté, uncovered, for 20 minutes, stir frequently.
Add carrot & garlic and cook 5 minutes longer.
Stir in mushrooms and cook 5 minutes.
Raise heat to moderate; stir in wine, salt, rosemary and sage.
Place pork chops on top and cover, cook for 4 minutes.
Turn chops over, cover and cook for 4 minutes longer.
Simmer for 20 minutes longer or until done.
Spoon mixture evenly on top of each chop.
Serve immediately. Serves 4

Grandpa in San Francisco in the 1920's - Grandpa in Nuoro, Sardinia, 1975

Spaghetti alla Genovese

Ingredients

2 bunches fresh parsley, removed from stems and finely chopped
6 cloves garlic – chopped
½ cup olive oil
¾ lb Spaghetti
Grated cheese, to taste

❧ Combine parsley, garlic and olive oil; set aside.
Cook Spaghetti al dente.
Mix together – add additional olive oil if needed.
Add grated cheese to taste.
Serves 4

Lasagna

Ingredients
1 lb sausage (out of casing and crumbled)
1 lb ground beef (crumbled)
3 cups tomato sauce
1 lb. Lasagna – uncooked (I usually make extra)
4 cups (2 lbs) whole milk ricotta cheese
2 cups (8-oz) shredded whole milk mozzarella cheese (Polly-O)
¼ cup grated Romano cheese
4 eggs
1 Tbsp chopped fresh parsley
1 tsp salt
¼ tsp ground black pepper

❧ Brown meat in 3-quart saucepan; drain fat (brown sausage and beef separately). Set aside
Cook Lasagna according to package directions; pour cold water in pot to make it easier to handle.
Combine cheeses, eggs, parsley, salt & pepper for filling.
Pour about ½ cup sauce on bottom of 13" x 9" baking pan.
Arrange 4 pieces of lasagna lengthwise over sauce.
Spread 1/3 of the cheese filling over lasagna and cover with ground beef, sausage and sauce.
Repeat layers of lasagna, cheese, sauce and meat until pan is full.
Pour sauce on top and sprinkle with Romano cheese.
Bake at 350° degrees, about 45 minutes or until hot and bubbly. Serves 6 - 8

Mom's communion (Anna) with Aunt Elizabeth at Our Lady of Mount Carmel Church in Manhattan

Macaroni & Cheese

Ingredients
½ lb elbow macaroni
1 8-oz package of Velveeta cheese, cut into small cubes
2 Tbsp butter
2 Tbsp flour
¼ tsp salt
1/8 tsp pepper
1 cup milk

❧ Cook macaroni al dente; drain; pour into baking dish.
Melt butter over low heat in a heavy saucepan. (Wooden spoon for stirring is best)
Blend in flour, seasonings, cook over low heat, stirring until mixture is smooth and bubbly.
Remove from heat.
Stir in milk and ½ the cheese.
Place pan back on heat and bring to boil – stirring constantly for 1 minute.
Pour sauce over macaroni and mix well.
Cover with remaining cheese. Bake at 350° until cheese is melted (not too long).
Serves 4

Vinnie & Tom on Christmas Eve

Vinnie's Scarpariello

Ingredients

1 whole chicken, cut up
6 Italian sausage links – 3 hot and 3 sweet
1 large onion, diced
1 ripe tomato, diced
1 stalk celery, diced
5 or 6 big cloves garlic, minced
Paprika
Salt
Pepper
Red wine

❧ Coat chicken with oil, salt, pepper and paprika; place in large baking pan.
Add tomato, onion, celery and garlic on top of chicken; drizzle with red wine.
Bake in 350° oven for about 1 hour.
Turn chicken over; adding more seasoning and wine.
Bake for ½ hour and add sausage.
Cook ½ hour longer, or until sausage is cooked through.

Serves 4

Santo with his sisters Tina and Angelina

Cauliflower with Macaroni

Ingredients

1 large cauliflower, cut into florets
4 Tbsp olive oil
6 cloves fresh garlic, minced
4 heaping Tbsp grated cheese (Parmigiano or Pecorino Romano)
Salt & pepper, to taste
¾ lb pasta (Ziti or Rigatoni)

❧ In a large pasta pot, place cauliflower; cover with water – almost to top of pot; add pinch of salt; boil until very tender.
While cauliflower is cooking, sauté garlic in oil until slightly brown; set aside in large serving bowl.
When cauliflower is tender, remove with a small strainer or slotted spoon – reserve water.
Mix with garlic, add oil and cheese and mash together.
Bring reserved water to a boil - add more if needed - cook pasta until done to taste.
Add pasta to mixture and serve.
-Can be reheated if leftover
Serves 4

Lentil Soup

Ingredients

½ lb dried lentils – examine, sort & rinse well
1 ½ cups chopped celery
1 ½ cups chopped onion
1 ½ cups chopped carrots
4 cloves garlic – chopped finely
1 bay leaf
1 center cut Ham slice (approximately 1 to 1 ¼ lbs – diced (remove and set aside skin and fat)
¼ cup Olive oil
½ tsp dried basil
Salt & pepper to taste
2 16-oz cans chicken broth
2 cans water
1 cup dry red wine (optional)

In heavy 8 quart stockpot heat oil, add ham skin, fat, garlic, onion, basil, carrots, celery, bay leaf, salt and pepper. Sauté until vegetables are tender.

Remove all pieces of ham skin from pot.

Add diced ham pieces and sauté for 2 minutes.
Add 2 cans chicken broth, 2 cans water and wine – bring to boil.
Add lentils (remove bay leaf) and simmer for 45 minutes or until lentils are tender. Stir occasionally.

Serve as is or with elbow macaroni.

Note: Add water as necessary for desired thickness

Alex at his Communion

Spaghetti with Shrimp & Asparagus

Ingredients

¾ lb Spaghetti
1 lb Shrimp (defrosted raw w/tail 21-25 count shrimp) (or fresh cleaned)
¼ cup Olive Oil
4 cloves garlic chopped (more or less to taste)
1 bunch Asparagus – snapped into 3 pieces (discard the end)
(You can use Broccoli instead or Asparagus or no vegetables at all)

❧ Start water for spaghetti.
Heat Olive oil and sauté garlic in pan on medium heat for 2 – 3 minutes.
Add Asparagus and sauté 6 – 7 minutes until tender (as desired).
Add shrimp & sauté in single layer about 2 – 3 minutes turn and sauté another 2 – 3 minutes or until pink.
When shrimp is almost done check spaghetti – if done drain and add to shrimp/asparagus mixture and toss.
If spaghetti is not done when shrimp mixture is done, take shrimp mixture off heat.
Add salt, pepper and Parmesan cheese to taste. (We use Locatelli Pecorino Romano)
Serve with Italian Bread and a Green Salad.

Serves 2 - 4

Tom at the beach in Alghero, Italy

<u>Rack of Lamb</u>

2 Fresh Racks of Lamb (approx. 8 chops each)

❧Sprinkle lamb with rosemary, pepper and basil, coat with extra virgin olive and rub into lamb, sprinkle with spices again, do this on both sides of lamb. Put in refrigerator for at least an hour to marinate before cooking.
Broil for approximately 7 minutes on each side. Do not overcook.
Serves 4

Steamed Maryland Blue Claw Crabs

Ingredients
2 dozen "live" blue claw male crabs
1 cup red apple cider vinegar
1 cup water
1 cup beer

Mix together
4-oz old bay
4-oz coarse kosher salt
1 tsp ground red pepper

In large steam pot put vinegar, water and beer and bring to boil. In steamer basket layer crabs, sprinkling with old bay mixture. Cover and steam until crabs are cooked. (you will know the crabs are cooked when they turn red) Do not over cook. Approximately 15 minutes.
Serve with vinegar and old bay or melted butter

Note: If crabs are dead throw away – do not use
Serves 4

Grilled Hot Sausage and Peppers

Ingredients
3 Andouille Sausages
3 Chorizo sausages
3 Hot Italian sausages
2 red bell peppers
2 green bell peppers
2 yellow bell peppers
1 large Vidalia onion
¼ cup balsamic vinegar
1/8 cup extra virgin olive oil
½ tsp oregano
½ tsp basil
Salt
Pepper

Wash, remove seeds and stem from peppers – cut in quarters.
Clean onion – cut in quarters

Put peppers and onion in large boil with balsamic Vinegar, extra virgin olive oil, oregano, basil, salt and pepper to taste and marinate for at least 1 hour.
Grill sausages on low heat for ½ hour or until done.
Grill peppers and onion in grilling basket stirring frequently on low heat for ½ hour or until peppers are tender with slight charring.
Mix sausages and peppers together (slice sausages and peppers if desired).
Serves 4

Grits with Gouda Cheese and Italian Sausage

Ingredients
1 cup grits
4 1/4 cups water
2 Tbsp. butter
Salt to taste
2 links mild Italian sausage
1 cup shredded Gouda cheese
Olive oil

Cook Grits

Add water, grits, butter and salt to sauce pan, mix and bring to boil. Reduce heat and simmer for 45 minutes. (if grits is a little soupy that is fine) (if grits are dry add a little water)

Remove casing from sausage, crumble and fry in olive oil until done approximately 20 minutes, turning constantly. Drain oil and set aside.

When grits are done mix in cheese and sausage. Put in baking dish and bake @ 350° for 45 minutes. Stir once at 20 minutes.

Can be served for breakfast or as a side dish for dinner.

Service 6

Eggplant, Mozzarella & Portabella Mushroom Pannini

Ingredients
1 Loaf Organic Rosemary Boule (or any artisan bread)
1 lb. Fresh whole milk Mozzarella cheese, sliced
1 Eggplant
4 Portabella mushrooms
Olive oil
Basil
Oregano
Garlic powder
Pepper

❧ Wash and slice eggplant approximately ¼" thick, drizzle olive oil on eggplant and sprinkle with oregano, basil, garlic powder, pepper (add whatever spices you prefer).

❧ Wash Portabella mushrooms – rub with olive oil, sprinkle with basil, oregano and pepper.

❧ Grill eggplant on low flame until soft and browned about 15 minutes turning at least once.
Grill mushrooms on low flame until tender turning regularly.

❧ Slice bread approximately ½" thick (8 slices) layer cheese, eggplant, mushroom cheese. Brush outside of bread with olive oil.

❧ Grill on low flame until bread is toasted turn once. (this is very quick)

Serves 4

Chicken Cutlet Parmigiano

Ingredients
2 lbs. Thin sliced chicken breasts
2 eggs
Seasoned breadcrumbs
Olive oil – fill frying pan approximately ¼" deep
Tomato sauce (see page 37, omit meat)
16 oz. whole milk Mozzarella cheese, sliced
Grated Pecorino Romano cheese to taste

❧ Dip chicken breasts in egg and then in breadcrumbs to coat. Fry in olive oil on medium heat for approximately 8 minutes on each side until golden brown. Drain on paper towel.

❧ In large baking dish arrange one layer of chicken, spread tomato sauce over chicken and layer with mozzarella cheese, spread tomato sauce over cheese and sprinkle with grated Pecorino Romano cheese.

❧ Bake @ 350° approximately 20 minutes until cheese is melted.

Serves 4

Mary Manca

Side Dishes

Josephine's Spinach Pie

Stuffed Calamari

8 – nice size calamari bodies washed and turned inside out – remove any spine.
(do this carefully as they break very easily)
Prepare 1 recipe of plain tomato sauce, simmer while preparing calamari.

Filling
2 cups flavored breadcrumb
½ cup grated cheese (we use Pecorino Romano)
1 16-oz. can tomato sauce
1 clove garlic – chopped
2 Tbsp. Olive oil

❦ Sauté garlic in oil.
Pour in breadcrumb, add enough sauce to make them moist, add cheese and sauté, mix well.
Cool mixture
Fill calamari ¾ full; use a toothpick to keep mixture in.
Place into simmering sauce and cook for ½ hour.
Serve with spaghetti / Serves 4

Josephine's Spinach Pie

Mary Jo & Russ

Ingredients

Sweet Dough (Pasta Frolla')
2 cups flour
1 Tbsp sugar
1 tsp baking powder
1 beaten egg in ¾ cup cold water
2 Tbsp salad oil or melt 2 Tbsp Oleo or butter
1/8 tsp salt

❧ Place sifted dry ingredients into large bowl - add wet ingredients - blend together, this is a slightly sticky dough. Form into a ball. Have patience - it will come together.
On lightly floured board knead lightly (about 10x).
Add flour to board or it will stick - Place in oiled bowl. Make a cross on top (My mother used to then say "crescere figlia bella" (grow my lovely daughter). She had 6 daughters. Cover, place in warm place for 1/2 hour - again flour board - cut 3/4 of dough and roll out to form 9" circle for pie pan, save 1/4 dough for lattice strips cut in 1" for top.

❧ Hint: Roll pie dough on floured wax paper - easy to transfer to pie plate.
Bake shell for 10 minutes at 375°.

Spinach Filling
1 lb spinach or 2 - 10 oz. boxes frozen spinach, boil, drain, and chop fine.
Place spinach in bowl and add 1 15oz container ricotta or 2 cups, 1 beaten egg, 1 Tbsp flour, 1/4 cup shredded mozzarella, 1/4 cup parmesan cheese, 1/2 tsp garlic powder, 1/4 tsp black pepper, 1/4 tsp cinnamon.
❧ Pour mixed filling into baked pie shell - top with lattice strips (criss-cross).
Bake at 375° for 10 minutes, than bake at 325° for 30 minutes
Insert knife in center - check if dried.
Remove from oven. Cool and serve. Serves 6 – 8

<u>Stuffed Clams</u>

Ingredients

12 Cherrystone clams
3 cloves garlic
3-oz olive oil
1 8-oz bottle clam juice
1 cup breadcrumbs (flavored)
Grated Romano cheese

❧ Wash and open clams, reserving clam juice and shells
Chop Clams
Chop garlic and put in the oil.
Mix chopped clams with breadcrumb and clam juice
Dry shells and add some mixture to each one
You will probably only fill about 16 shells.
Add a drizzle of oil to each holding back the garlic, and a drizzle of clam juice.
Sprinkle with cheese and bake at 350° for 20 minutes.
Check often, do not let them get dry.
Keep putting a little oil and clam juice on them.
Serves 6

Steamed Clams

Ingredients

3 dozen little neck clams
1 8-oz bottle clam juice
1 head of garlic
½ cup olive oil
½ cup white wine
1 stick butter
Juice from ½ lemon
Fresh parsley to taste

Slice garlic very thin and sauté until soft in olive oil. Add white wine, lemon juice, clam juice and butter, simmer until butter is melted. Add clams and simmer until all clams are open, add parsley.
Serve in large bowl with warm crusty Italian bread.
Serves 4

Vienna's Sausage Stuffing

For 20 lb Turkey

Ingredients
3 lbs Sausage
1 loaf Italian bread
Fresh Parsley –chopped, to taste, but not to much
1 clove garlic - minced
1 16-oz package of Mozzarella – cut in small cubes
Grated cheese – to taste
Salt – to taste
Pepper – a little
2 eggs – beaten

❦ Put a little oil in a pan. Remove the sausage from it's casing and crumble into pan. Sauté until done, about 15 minutes. (There shouldn't be any liquid left in the pan, but don't burn it)
Let it cool.
Cut off the crust of the bread and soak in warm water. Squeeze out all the liquid really well. In a bowl add sausage, bread, parsley, garlic, mozzarella, grated cheese, salt and pepper, mix well.
Add the eggs just before stuffing the turkey or just before baking the stuffing.

❦ The stuffing must be completely cooled before adding the eggs. If the stuffing is made ahead of time, do not add the eggs until ready to use/bake. Bake for approximately 1 hour or until heated through.

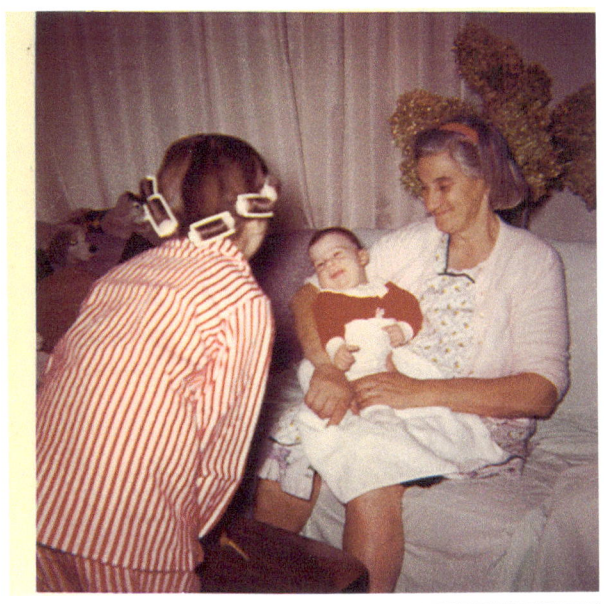
Grandma holding Tommy with Mary Ann making him laugh at Christmas time

Potato Croquettes

2 cups mashed potatoes
1 Tbsp parsley
2 Tbsp grated cheese
3 Tbsp grated mozzarella
1 egg separated
2 Tbsp milk
Pepper to taste
1 cup breadcrumb (seasoned)

◈ Mix all ingredients except milk & egg white.
Form into palm size ball and flatten to an oval shape.
Mix egg white & milk together.
Dip in egg white and then in breadcrumb, repeat if too soft.
Fry in hot oil until golden brown
Remove carefully.

We usually make this with leftover mashed potatoes.
Serves 4

Ollie's Potato Salad

Ingredients

10 lbs potatoes
1 large onion – diced
2 to 3 small sweet pickles – diced very small (save juice)
6 hard boiled eggs – chopped fine with yolks
¼ cup vegetable oil
½ cup miracle whip (or mayonnaise)
1 Tbsp yellow mustard – to taste
4 stalks celery – finely diced
Celery seeds – very little - optional
Salt & pepper to taste

❧ Cook potatoes with skin on until done but firm.
Cool potatoes
Peel all potatoes – cut into 3/4" cubes
Combine potatoes in large bowl with onion, eggs, sweet pickles, and celery.
Mix oil with pickle juice, then pour onto potato mixture and let marinate for ½ hour – stir occasionally.
Then add Miracle whip and yellow mustard – mix till all potatoes are coated.
Add celery seeds, salt and pepper while mixing to taste.

❧ Add more Miracle Whip if needed
Serves 10 - 12

Seafood Salad

Ingredients
2 ½ lbs of cleaned squid (tubes & tentacles)
1 lb Medium shrimp
1 lb Scallops
1 lb Mussels – optional
1 6-oz can large pitted ripe black olives
5 cloves garlic
Olive oil
3 stalks celery
5 lemons
Salt & pepper

∾ Cut squid into small pieces and put into boiling water.
Clean shrimp and cut in half.
Put shrimp and scallops in with squid.
When water comes back to a boil remove and strain and let cool.
Coat seafood with olive oil.
Slice olives and celery and add to seafood.
Chop garlic and add to seafood.
Squeeze juices from lemons and add to seafood.
Salt and pepper to taste.
Mix thoroughly.
Prepare 4 or 5 hours ahead of time and mix occasionally.
Serve chilled
Serves 8

Polpo (left) & Seafood Salad (right)

<u>Polpo</u>

Ingredients
1 large octopus
6 quarts water in large pot
Pinch of salt

⊱ Bring water to boil
With a big fork lift octopus and dip it 3 times then leave in pot.
Cook unit tender – test with fork, when fork comes out easy it is done.
Remove to a colander and remove pink skin and cups.
Clean head and rinse.
Cut in 1-inch pieces.

Mix with ¼ cup oil
Juice of 2 lemons
Sprig of parsley
2 cloves of garlic

Serve cold
Serves 2 - 4

Grandpa holding a bee's nest in the apple orchard on the farm

Whiting Salad (fish)

Ingredients
2 nice size whiting (cleaned)
3 cloves garlic
Sprig of parsley
Juice of 3 lemons
2 Tbsp olive oil

❧ Poach whiting in boiling water for 15 minutes.
Do not over cook!
Skin and bone.
Shred and mix with other ingredients.
Serves 2 - 4

*Nan (Anna) & Kerry (Anna's Granddaughter) in front of the Fugazi Building in San Francisco, California
Grandpa helped with the construction of this building when he was in San Francisco in the 1920's*

<u>Asparagus</u>

*❧ I use two bunches of Asparagus
Boil until tender – not to soft
Drain*

Slice two garlic cloves

Arrange in plate and drizzle olive oil over Asparagus, mix in sliced garlic.

Beef Braciola

Ingredients

2 packages of 2 pieces each round steak cut for braciola
1 cup flavored breadcrumbs
1 8-oz can tomato sauce
2 Tbsp grated Romano cheese
4 Tbsp olive oil
2 cloves garlic – chopped
1 Tbsp parsley flakes

Sauté garlic in 2 Tbsp olive oil, add tomato sauce and cook for 5 minutes – turn stove off.
Add enough breadcrumbs to soak up sauce, add cheese and parsley – mix well.

Lay braciola flat on board, spread mixture over ¾ of braciola and roll tight. Tie together with cooking string.

Sauté braciola in 2 Tbsp olive oil until brown.
Add to your traditional tomato sauce while it's simmering for at least ½ hour.
Serves 2 - 4

Aunt Marie's son Ronnie

Onions for Hot Dogs

Ingredients

3 sliced onions
1 8-oz can tomato sauce
Salt
Pepper

ఈ *Fry onions in a little oil, add tomato sauce, salt & pepper – simmer till done.*

Cousin Andy loved anything Grandma cooked!

Italian Potato Salad

Ingredients

1 ½ lbs baby red potatoes
1 Vidalia onion or red onion - cut up
5 Tbsp oil
2 Tbsp vinegar

ઈ Boil potatoes until tender but firm, cool and peel.
Slice potatoes and mix with onion, oil, vinegar, salt & pepper.
Serve warm or cold
Serves 2 - 4

Grandma's Potato & Eggs

Ingredients

4 large potatoes, peeled and sliced
Oil
3 eggs
Salt to taste

❧ In a large skillet, fry potatoes in oil until golden brown.
Salt potatoes, to taste.
Drain oil.
Beat 3 eggs in a bowl and pour over potatoes.
After mixture is set, cover with a dinner plate and flip (over the sink).
Cook on other side until done.

Good served with chicken soup and Italian bread

Serves 4

The family at Grandpa's "77th" birthday

__Giambotta__

Ingredients

1 medium onion, chopped
2 medium zucchini, peeled and cubed
1 large potato, cubed
Sprig of fresh basil or 1 tsp dried basil
Salt & pepper, to taste
1 8-oz can tomato sauce
3 Tbsp oil
½ cup water

❧ Sauté onion in oil until golden.
Add 8-oz can tomato sauce, simmer 5 minutes.
Add potato, zucchini and basil, cook 10 minutes.
Add water.
Bring to a slow boil; lower heat; cook until tender.
Serve with warm, crusty Italian bread

Serves 2

Broccoli Rabe

Ingredients

2 bunches Broccoli Rabe – cleaned, washed and trimmed
¼ cup olive oil
3 cloves garlic, sliced
4 quarts water
Salt to taste
Pepper to taste
Red pepper flakes, to taste

❧ Place broccoli in pot of water and boil until tender, but not over cooked. (better under cooked than over cooked). Drain.
Heat oil; sauté garlic until golden brown.
Add salt, pepper, pepper flakes and broccoli to pan.

Toss and Serve. / Serves 4

*A typical weekend on the farm
(from left to right – Sam, Grandma, Cousin Andy, Grandpa
top – Uncle Mike and Marty)*

Fried Cauliflower

Ingredients

1 large head cauliflower, washed and cut into florets
½ cup grated cheese (Pecorino Romano)
3 eggs
½ cup milk
2 cups flavored breadcrumbs
1 cup of oil
Salt and pepper

❧ Boil cauliflower in large pot of water, until tender – do not over cook; drain.
Beat together eggs, milk and cheese.
Dip florets in egg mixture; then in breadcrumbs.
Fry in oil until golden brown.
Add salt & pepper to taste.
Serves 4

Rice Stuffing

Ingredients

1 cup uncooked white rice
1 small onion – diced
2 Tbsp Olive oil
1 liver from chicken or turkey – chopped
4 Tbsp grated cheese (Parmigiano or Pecorino Romano)
6 Tbsp butter
2 Tbsp chopped fresh parsley
Salt & pepper to taste

❧ Cook rice

❧ In small sauce pan sauté onion in olive oil until golden - add liver, salt, pepper and parsley. Sauté for approximately 10 minutes or until liver is tender.

❧ Put cooked rice in a baking dish add butter, grated cheese and liver mixture – mix well.

Bake 20 minutes and serve.

Serves 4

Stuffed Peppers

Ingredients

6 Italian (green) peppers (also called Cubanelles)
2 cups flavored breadcrumbs
½ cup grated Italian cheese (Pecorino Romano)
1 16-oz can tomato sauce
1 clove garlic, chopped
2 Tbsp oil
Oil for frying

❧ Sauté garlic in 2 tablespoons oil.
Pour in breadcrumbs, tomato sauce (just enough to make them moist) and cheese; sauté until well mixed.
Cool mixture.
Wash peppers, cut off tops and reserve them, clean out seeds.
Spoon mixture into each pepper.
Replace pepper tops and secure with toothpicks.
Fry stuffed peppers in oil until cooked on all sides.
Serves 6

Andrea's Granddaughter Isabella

Broccoli Casserole

Ingredients

2 10-oz boxes frozen chopped broccoli, cooked, drained.
1 stick salted butter
½ lb Velveeta cheese
¼ lb Ritz crackers, crushed

❦ Cook and drain broccoli
Add ½ stick butter and cheese to broccoli.
Place broccoli and cheese mixture in buttered baking dish.
Cover broccoli with crushed crackers.
Melt remaining ½ stick butter and drizzle over crumbs.
Bake at 350° for about 30 minutes.
Serves 4 - 6

Pasta Salad, Cucumber Salad & Barbequed Chicken

Aunt Marie's Pasta Salad

Ingredients

1 16-oz bottle Zesty Italian dressing
1 lb tri-color Rotelli pasta, cooked
1 6-oz can large pitted ripe black olives, chopped
½ lb Feta cheese
1 4-oz jar pimento peppers, chopped
1 small onion, chopped
Salt and pepper, to taste
Grating cheese – small handful

❧ Add all ingredients together and refrigerate until ready to be served
Serves 6

Julia & Katie (Aunt Marie's Granddaughters)

Aunt Marie's Corn Pudding

Ingredients

1 15.2-oz can corn kernels
1 cup milk
2 eggs, beaten
2 Tbsp flour
3 Tbsp sugar
Salt & pepper to taste
Butter

❧ Mix all ingredients together, except for butter.
Pour into greased baking pan.
Butter top of mixture.
Bake at 350° for 45 minutes.
Serves 4

Michele and Bob in Florence Italy

Panzanella – Bread Salad and One Other Summer Dish

Ingredients

2 large tomatoes, seeded and cut into ½ inch cubes
¼ cup fresh basil, chopped
1-2 Tbsp capers
½ cup extra virgin olive oil
¼ cup red wine vinegar
3 cucumbers, peeled, halved, seeded and cut in ½ inch cubes
1 small red onion, peeled and thinly sliced
1 bell pepper (any color), cored, seeded and cut into thin strips
Salt and fresh ground pepper, to taste
½ loaf day old country bread (a loaf of good French or Italian bead can be substituted)

❦ In a small bowl, combine the tomatoes, basil, capers, oil, vinegar, salt and pepper.
Cut the bread into ½ inch thick cubes.
Place the bread on a platter or in a shallow bowl.
Scatter the cucumbers, onion and bell pepper over the bread.
Sprinkle the tomato mixture over the bread mixture and toss.
Can be served immediately, an hour later at room temperature or refrigerated and served the next day - after bringing to room temperature (if the salad is too dry, add additional oil and vinegar). Serves 4

Fresh Mozzarella, Tomatoes and Basil Salad

Ingredients

1 lb fresh Mozzarella, cut into thin slices.
2 or 3 ripe tomatoes, cut into thin slices
¼ cup fresh basil, chopped
Balsamic vinegar
Extra virgin olive oil
Salt and pepper, to taste

❧ Layer the mozzarella and tomatoes in a serving dish; alternating the slices in a fan shape.
Sprinkle with basil, then balsamic vinegar, and finally olive oil.
Add salt and pepper, to taste.
Serve at room temperature.
Serves 2 - 4

Orange Salad

Ingredients

1 head red romaine lettuce – washed and broken into bite size pieces
1 head green romaine lettuce – washed and broken into bite size pieces
1 large red onion - sliced
5 oranges – peeled and separated into slices

Mix together for dressing:
2/3 cup olive oil
1/3 cup Tarragon vinegar
1 tsp sugar
Salt and pepper to taste
Paprika to taste

❧ In large bowl add lettuce, onion and oranges and mix together.

❧ When ready to serve pour dressing mixture over lettuce and mix together.

Serves 6

Cucumber Salad

Ingredients

1 cup sugar
1 cup water
1 cup vinegar
1 Vidalia onion – sliced
Salt and pepper to taste
6 cucumbers

❧ I like to peel my cucumbers but you don't have to – to make the cucumber look a little fancier you can score the cucumber by running the tines of a fork lengthwise down each cucumber, go around the whole cucumber.

Slice cucumbers into a colander sprinkling with salt as you go.

In a serving bowl add cucumbers, water, sugar, vinegar, salt and pepper to taste and mix together.

Serve chilled

Serves 6

Tortellini & Spinach Salad

Ingredients

1 16-oz package tri color cheese filled Tortellini
1 medium size Vidalia onion – chopped
1 16-oz package fresh spinach – washed and remove stems
1 14-oz can artichoke hearts – quartered
1 3 ½-oz package sun dried tomatoes – chopped
½ cup sliced black olives (optional)
1 4-oz package crumbled feta cheese
1 Tbsp dried or fresh parsley
½ cup olive oil
¼ cup lemon juice
¼ cup red wine vinegar
Salt & pepper to taste

❧ Cook Tortellini al dente as per package.

In a large bowl mix olive oil, lemon juice, red wine vinegar, salt & pepper. Add Tortellini and coat well. Stir in remaining ingredients except spinach. Refrigerate. Add spinach and toss before serving.

Serves 6

Aunt Elizabeth & Uncle Mal in the 1920's

All Holidays

Antipasto for Holidays

Ingredients

½ large head iceberg lettuce - chopped
1 bunch celery - chopped
1 6-oz can large black olives – pitted and drained, halved
1 16-oz jar green olives stuffed with pimento – drained, halved
1 32-oz jar sweet vinegar peppers – drained, chopped
1 2-oz can anchovies – flat
2 Tbsp olive oil

❧ Chop first five ingredients mix together in a bowl with olive oil.
Place in serving dish.
Arrange anchovies on top; pour excess oil from anchovies over the mixture.
Serves 8 - 10

The family picnic in Theisi, Sardinia

Roasted Peppers

Ingredients

6 large red bell peppers
6 cloves garlic
4 Tbsp olive oil
Salt & pepper, to taste

Bake peppers on cookie sheet in hot oven (425° to 450°) until skin starts to turn black. (Turn occasionally to cook evenly - DO NOT puncture with fork, use oven mitt or potholder when turning)
When done, place evenly in a large paper bag that is placed in a plastic bag (you should do this in the sink).
Tie bags tightly, wait five minutes.
Take out 1 pepper at a time and place in a colander - have cold water running slowly outside of colander.
Peel skin and remove seeds from peppers, rinse hands and peppers off, when not too hot, and cut into strips.
Mix with garlic, olive oil, salt and pepper to taste.
Serve at room temperature.
Serves 4

Caponata

Ingredients

2 cups eggplant, peeled and cubed
1 tsp kosher salt
4 Tbsp olive oil
1 cup red onion, chopped
½ cup green bell pepper, chopped
½ cup red pepper, chopped
¾ cup chopped, celery
2 cups drained canned plum tomatoes, chopped (keep juice)
½ tsp black pepper
½ tsp oregano
½ tsp dried basil
1 Tbsp chopped garlic cloves
1 Tbsp chopped fresh parsley
½ cup Calamata olives, chopped
½ cup balsamic vinegar

❧ Place eggplant in colander; sprinkle with salt and let drain for 1 hour.
Heat 2 tsp oil in large saucepan.
Pat eggplant dry and sauté 10 minutes or until light brown - remove eggplant.
Add remaining oil, onion, peppers and celery and sauté 10 minutes.
Return eggplant to pan.
Add tomatoes, pepper, oregano, basil, garlic, parsley and olives.
Add balsamic vinegar to mixture.
Simmer 45 minutes or until tender.

* If it begins to stick to pan, add juice from tomatoes

Serves 6 - 8

Rice Balls (Arancini)

Ingredients

1 cup rice, uncooked
¼ lb ground beef
2 Tbsp olive oil
1 clove garlic, minced
½ small onion, chopped
¼ lb mushrooms (½ small can)
2 Tbsp tomato paste
1 cup warm water
¼ tsp salt
¼ tsp pepper
½ cup butter
3 Tbsp grated cheese
2 egg yolks
1 egg beaten
1 cup breadcrumbs
1 cup olive oil
Raisins & pignoli nuts

❧ Cook rice.
While rice is cooking - place ground beef, oil, garlic, and onion in saucepan and brown gently.
Add mushrooms; cook 1 minute.
Add tomato paste and water; simmer on low heat for 30 minutes; add salt and pepper.
To cooked rice; add butter and cheese; cool.
After cooled, add egg yolks and tomato gravy to rice (holding aside the meat and mushrooms in a strainer); mix well.
Make little balls of rice - placing inside each ball – 1 tsp reserved meat, mushrooms, a couple of raisins and nuts.
Dip rice balls into beaten egg; roll in breadcrumbs.
Using a deep skillet, fry rice balls in hot oil until golden brown all over.
Serves 6

Stuffed Mushrooms

Stuffed Mushrooms & Caponata

Ingredients

12 large mushrooms, remove stems
1 tsp parsley
2 cloves garlic – chopped
1 cup breadcrumbs- flavored
Shredded Mozzarella, optional
Salt & pepper
4 Tbsp grated cheese
½ stick melted butter
Olive oil

❧ Mix parsley, garlic, breadcrumbs, salt, pepper, grated cheese and melted butter together.
Stuff mushrooms.
Sprinkle top of mushrooms with mozzarella (optional).
Grease a baking sheet with oil or Pam.
Place mushrooms on sheet and sprinkle with olive oil.
Bake until breadcrumbs browned on top.
If too dry, add oil.
Try not to overcook.
Serves 6

Stuffed Artichokes

Ingredients
6 large artichokes
2 cups flavored breadcrumb
½ cup grated cheese
6 cloves garlic –chopped
½ cup fresh parsley – chopped
½ cup olive oil

Wash and remove any dry leaves from artichoke.
Cut off stalks so that they will sit upright in pan.
Cut one inch off the top.
Spread and remove core especially if it is purple and spiny.
Mix well breadcrumb, cheese, 4 chopped garlic cloves and ¼ cup chopped parsley.
Spoon mixture into artichokes spreading leaves as you go. Use up all mixture.

In a sauce pan large enough to hold 6 artichokes close together and deep enough to fill with water ¾ of the height. Place artichokes in pot, drizzle artichokes with oil. Add remaining oil, garlic and parsley to water in pot.
Cook until tender and leaf pulls off easily. Serves 6

Eggplant Parmigiano

I usually use two eggplants for an 8 x 8 x 2 baking dish.

(2) Eggplant
Seasoned breadcrumbs as needed
2 Eggs
Romano grated cheese
1 16-oz Mozzarella cheese
Tomato sauce

❧ Start your tomato sauce (see page 33 – omit meat)

❧ Peal eggplant and Cut in approximately 1/8" slices
Dip eggplant in egg and then in breadcrumbs.
Fry in hot olive oil until lightly golden and drain on paper towel
Place in baking dish with layers of eggplant, mozzarella cheese, sprinkle with Romano cheese and then sauce, do this until dish is full.
Then Bake until hot.
Or freeze before baking for another day.
Serves 6

Breads

Gino & Carlo Bar in San Francisco, California where Grandpa hung out in the 1920's

Irish Soda Bread

Ingredients

4 cups flour
2 tsp baking powder
1 tsp salt
1 stick salted butter
1 cup sugar
1 cup raisins

In bowl combine flour, baking powder, salt and sugar, cut in butter with pastry knife until smooth – add raisins.

In another bowl mix
1 1/3 cups buttermilk
2 eggs
1 tsp baking soda.

Add together and knead until smooth.
Bake 350° about 50 minutes

Makes 2 loaves bread

Braided Easter Bread

Ingredients

6 cups flour + 2 cups for board
1 Tbsp oil
1/3 cup sugar
½ cup warm water
½ tsp salt
2 eggs beaten
¼ tsp cinnamon
Place 1 package dry yeast in ½ cup warm water with 1 tsp sugar for 10 minutes

❧ In large bowl, sift 6 cups flour, sugar and salt - add ¼ cup warm water and 1 Tbsp oil - add in yeast mixture.
Soft dough - turn onto lightly floured board - knead 5 minutes, until smooth.
Place in lightly oiled bowl to rise about 1 ½ hours - will double - can leave it overnight.
Punch down - knead in raisins and citron.
Divide into thirds - roll dough in palms to make 3 ropes.
Place ropes diagonally on greased cookie sheet - braid (like hair) pinch ends together and cover.
Let rise in a warm place for 1 hour.
Brush with egg white and color sprinkles if desired.
Bake 350° for 35 minutes until golden brown.
Tap with fingers tips - will sound hollow
Cool & serve
Traditional sweet bread for Easter Breakfast

Aunt Marie's Pumpkin Bread

Mix well dry ingredients

3 cups sugar
3 1/3 cup flour
1 tsp salt
2 tsp baking soda
2 tsp nutmeg
3 tsp cinnamon
½ tsp cloves
1 cup raisins
1 cup walnuts

Mix well
4 eggs
1 cup oil
2 cups pumpkin (1 small can 15 oz.)
2/3 cups water
Add to dry ingredients

Grease pans
2 bread pans 5 – 9
3 bread pans 4 x 8
Fill pans ½ way
Bake 325° 1 hour or until knife comes out clean

Easter Bread

Ingredients

7 cups flour   *Remove two cups of flour*
1 package yeast   *Add dry yeast*
½ cup sugar   *sugar*
1 tsp salt   *salt in a separate bowl*
2 cup warm water
¼ stick of salted butter
3 eggs

Melt butter in the 2 cups of warm water, add 5 cups of flour mix well, add to this the 2 cups flour mixed with dry yeast, sugar and salt mix well, then add your beaten eggs and mix well, if too moist just add a little flour, if dry wet your hand with warm water, this should not be sticky and should be easy to handle. Shape in a round ball and let rise 3 hours, cover with warm blanket.

Then punch down again and shape into one large loaf and place in a large pan well buttered and floured. Let rise again about 3 more hours. Brush top with butter.

Cook in oven 375° about ½ hour or as brown as you wish.

Tommy, Beauty and Andrea at the Farm

Desserts

Tom & Josie

Rugelach

Ingredients

2 cups flour
¼ tsp salt
1 cup melted salted butter
2 – 3 oz cream cheese
1/3 cup sour cream

- *Shape above ingredients into 4 disks and chill 2 hours or more*

- *Roll each disk in 9 inch rounds*
Mix together – ½ cup sugar & 1 tsp. cinnamon
Chop fine – ½ cup raisins and 1-cup walnuts then combine.
Press mix into dough
Cut each round into 12 wedges
Roll up
Chill 20 minutes

Bake at 350° – 22 minutes

Marianne's Nut Cookies
(Christmas Cookies)

Ingredients

½ lb salted butter
4 Tbsp sugar
2 tsp vanilla
2 cups flour
2 cups walnuts

❧ Mix by hand in bowl - put in nuts last.
Roll in small crescents and bake at 350° for 10 minutes after 10 minutes watch until browned.
Remove and cool.
Roll in sugar when cooled but not cold.

Jewel Cookies
(Christmas Cookies)

Ingredients
½ cup soft salted butter
¼ cup light brown sugar firmly packed
1 egg yolk
1 egg white slightly beaten
1 tsp vanilla
1 cup flour
1 cup finely chopped walnuts
Seedless red raspberry preserves

Makes about 24 cookies

❧ In medium bowl beat butter, sugar, vanilla and egg yolk with spoon until smooth, stir in flour till combined and refrigerate for 30 minutes.
Preheat oven 375°

❧ Roll dough into balls 1 inch in diameter.
Dip ball in egg white roll into walnuts and place each ball one inch apart on cookie sheet press center with thumb and bake 10 – 12 minutes or until lightly brown.
Remove and cool put preserves on top.

Bows
(Christmas Dessert)

Ingredients

4 egg yolks
¼ cup heavy cream (or milk)
1/3 cup sugar
1 2/3 cup sifted flour
¼ tsp salt
¼ tsp cinnamon
Powdered sugar (after cooked)

Beat egg yolks until light, add cream and sugar and beat well.
Add flour, salt and spice mix with hands.
Roll small amount of dough at a time to less then 1/8" thickness cut in 1" x 3" strips with pastry wheel cutting ends diagonally.
Make a long lengthwise slit in center of each strip and pull one end through.

Fry in hot deep fat (Crisco fat) at 350° for 2 minutes or until lightly browned turning once.
Drain on paper towel.
When cool sprinkle with powdered sugar.

Struffoli
(Christmas Dessert)

Ingredients

1 cup flour
2 tsp crisco
6 ½ tsp sugar
1 egg
1 ½ tsp. vanilla
2 Tbsp milk
1 pinch salt
1 ½ tsp. baking powder
1 pinch cinnamon

- *Double or triple recipe*

- *Sift dry ingredients, add wet ingredients and mix together with hands.*
Cut into strips and roll strips long ways with your hands (not a roller, you kind of want them to look like long cigars), cut into ½" pieces and then roll into balls.
Fry in oil until golden brown

- *For a triple batch use 1 cup honey, warmed in a pot on the stove, using a big slotted spoon dip Struffoli in honey and put in serving dish, sprinkle with colored non-perils (candy sprinkles). Arrange in round pie plates (we put paper doilies on the bottom of the pie plate for show).*
(1 cup flour makes 1 8" pie plate)

Tommy ready for the big game

Creamy Rice Pudding

Ingredients

1 cup cooked white rice
¼ tsp salt
¼ cup raisins (optional)
1 package vanilla pudding or pie filling
4 cups milk
1/3 cup sugar
1 egg (well beaten)
¼ tsp vanilla
1/8 tsp cinnamon
1/8 tsp nutmeg

Combine ingredients except vanilla and spices in saucepan. Cook and stir over medium heat until mixture comes to a full boil (8 to 10 minutes). Pour into bowl – sprinkle with cinnamon, nutmeg and vanilla. Serve warm or cold

Grandma A. with her 3 children Santo (Dad), Angelina & Tina

Grandma A. at her "100th" birthday with Santo & Angelina

Chocolate Pudding Pie

Ingredients

1 qt. whole milk
2 3.9-oz packages My T Fine chocolate pudding mix
½ 14.4-oz box graham crackers (Nabisco)
5 Tbsp salted butter - melted
½ cup granulated sugar

❧ *Place crackers in strong plastic baggie and crush with rolling pin until fine.*
Mix crushed graham crackers well with melted butter and sugar; if it seems to dry add more melted butter (1 Tbsp)
Pat ½ of crumbs in 9-inch Pyrex pie plate and bake at 350° for 10 minutes or till golden brown.
Make chocolate pudding according to instructions on box.
Pour into pie plate, let set 10 minutes, put remaining crumbs on top.

Bake for 10 minutes at 350°
Cool & refrigerate
Serves 6

Aunt Gertie and Uncle Mike at the farm

Italian Honey Twists
(Christmas & Easter Treat)

Ingredients
3 cups sifted flour
¼ cup sugar
1/8 tsp salt
2 Tbsp salted butter
1 tsp baking powder
6 Tbsp milk
3 eggs, slightly beaten
2 tsp grated lemon rind
8 drops of oil of anise or 1 tsp anise extract or 1 tsp vanilla
¼ cup honey, heated
10 x confectioner's powdered sugar

❧ Measure flour, ¼ cup sugar, baking powder and salt into sifter in a large bowl.
Scald milk with butter or Oleo in small pan.
Stir into dry mix
Add beaten eggs & lemon rind, oil of anise - mix to make stiff dough.
Knead until smooth on lightly floured board.
Roll out thin, ¼ at a time, cut with fluted pastry wheel into strips ¾" x 3" long - knot loosely and let stand 5 minutes to dry.

❧ Drop into deep fat heated to 375°, fry, and turn once - 2 - 3 minutes until golden - drain and cool.

❧ Sprinkle some with powdered sugar and some with warm honey and colored sprinkles for festive look.

Taralles

(Italian cookies with icing)

Ingredients

6 eggs lightly beaten
¼ lb salted butter melted and cooled
1 cup sugar
½ cup milk
1 tsp vanilla
6 tsp baking powder
5 cups flour

1. *Place beaten eggs in large bowl.*
   Add butter, sugar gradually mixing constantly with wooden spoon.

2. *Add milk, vanilla and baking powder and enough flour to make firm dough.*

3. *Flour your hands.*

4. *Break off a small piece of dough and roll into a sausage shape about ½ inch in diameter. Shape into a ring. Joining ends firmly.*

5. *Bake on a greased cookie sheet at 375° for 15 minutes.*

   Set aside.

   Icing
   2 cups confectioners' sugar
   4 – 6 Tbsp water
   1 tsp. Vanilla
   Colored sprinkles or sugar crystals (optional)

Combine sugar, water, and vanilla in a mixing bowl.
Dip cooled Taralles into icing or spread icing over them with fingers.
Top with sprinkles

The Assenzio Grandchildren

Pumpkin Pie

❧ *First take one large pumpkin – skin, gut and cube pumpkin.*
Boil pumpkin 1 – 2" cubes until tender.
Mash through colander.
Take what came through the colander and strain water out in very small strainer, take pumpkin that did not go through the strainer and put in measuring cup, until you have 2 cups of pumpkin.

2 eggs
2 cups pumpkin
¾ cup sugar
¼ tsp salt
1 tsp ground cinnamon
½ tsp ground ginger
¼ tsp ground cloves
1 2/3 cups evaporated milk

❧ *Heat oven to 425° prepare pastry for 1 9" pie crust. Beat eggs slightly with hand beater; beat in remaining ingredients. Place pastry-lined pie plate on oven rack; pour in filling. Bake 15 minutes.*
Reduce oven temperature to 350°. Bake until knife inserted in center comes out clean, 9 – inch pie 45 minutes longer; cool. Serve with Whipped Cream if desired.
Serves 6

Sock-it-to-me-Cake

Ingredients

1 package Duncan Hines Butter Recipe Golden Cake Mix
1 cup dairy sour cream
½ cup Crisco oil
¼ cup sugar
¼ cup water
4 eggs

Filling
1 cup chopped pecans
2 Tbsp brown sugar
2 tsp cinnamon

Preheat oven to 375°

❧ In large mixing bowl blend together the cake mix, sour cream, oil, ¼ cup sugar, water and eggs. Beat at high speed for 2 minutes. Pour 2/3 of the batter in a greased and floured 10-inch tube pan. Combine filling ingredients and sprinkle over batter in pan. Spread remaining batter evenly over filling mixture. Bake at 375° for 45 – 55 minutes, until cake springs back when touched lightly. Cool right side up for 25 minutes, then remove from pan.
Glaze: Blend 1-cup confectioner's sugar with 2 tbsp milk.
Drizzle over cake.

Makes 12 to 16 servings

Applesauce Cake

Ingredients

2 ½ cups flour
2 cups sugar
1 tsp salt
¼ tsp baking powder
1 ½ tsp baking soda
¾ tsp cinnamon
½ tsp cloves
½ tsp allspice
2 Tbsp cocoa
½ cup oil
¼ cup water
½ cup chopped walnuts
1 cup raisins
1 ½ cup applesauce
1 large egg

In large bowl, combine all dry ingredients, mixing until well blended. Add remaining ingredients and mix well. Pour all into 13 x 9 inch pan (greased).
Bake 45 minutes at 350°
Top with white icing or confectioners sugar

Grandpa and Aunt Marie sorting apples

Fresh Apple Pie

Ingredients

Pastry for 9-inch Two-Crust Pie
¾ cup sugar
¼ cup all purpose flour
½ tsp ground nutmeg
½ tsp ground cinnamon
Dash of salt
6 cups thinly sliced pared tart apples (about 6 medium)
2 Tbsp salted butter

Heat oven to 425°. Prepare pastry. Mix sugar, flour, nutmeg, cinnamon and salt. Stir in apples. Turn into pastry-lined pie plate; dot with butter. Cover with top crust that has slits cut in it; seal and flute. Cover edge with 3-inch strip of aluminum foil; remove foil during last 15 minutes of baking. Bake until crust is brown and juice begins to bubble through slits in crust, 40 to 50 minutes.
Serves 6

Some of Our Favorite Wines

Greg Norman – Cabernet Sauvignon – North Coast, California

Lyeth – Cabernet Sauvignon – Sonoma County, California

Simi – Cabernet Sauvignon – Alexander Valley, California

J. Lohr – Cabernet Sauvignon – Paso Robles, California

Bogle – Cabernet Sauvignon – Graton, California

Sterling – Cabernet Sauvignon – Calistoga, California

Santa Margarita – Pinot Grigio – Trentino - Alto Adige, Italy

Gallo Sonoma – Cabernet Sauvignon – Sonoma County, California

Stags Leap – Cabernet Sauvignon – Napa, California

Sassoaloaro – Cabernet – Tuscany Italy

Rodney Strong – Cabernet Sauvignon – Sonoma County, California

Silverado – Cabernet Sauvignon – Napa, California

Toasted Head – Cabernet Sauvignon & Merlot – Esparto, California

Wild Horses – Cabernet Sauvignon – Paso Robles, California

Ruffino – Chianti – Tuscany, Italy

Prager – Aria White Port – St. Helena, California

Grandpa's favorite – CK Barbarone

We hope you have enjoyed Our Family Favorites, please feel free to contact us at achaisson3@gmail.com if you have any questions or comments.

Happy Cooking!

www.ingramcontent.com/pod-product-compliance
Lightning Source LLC
Chambersburg PA
CBHW040911020526
44116CB00026B/30